Galapagos Islands Safari

by Grace Hansen

Abdo Kids Jumbo is an Imprint of Abdo Kids
abdobooks.com

Let's Go on Safari!

The Galapagos Islands are in the eastern Pacific Ocean. The islands are known for the special species that live there. Let's go on a Galapagos Islands safari!

North America
Pacific Ocean
Galapagos Islands
South America
Ecuador

A safari is a tour where people can see wild animals in their **habitats**. There are many ways to go on safari in the Galapagos Islands. Some people go by foot or by Jeep. Others go on safari by boat.

Galapagos Animals

Marine iguanas are special reptiles found only in the Galapagos. They are also the only lizards that swim in the sea. They feed underwater on **algae**.

Giant tortoises can weigh nearly 1,000 pounds (453 kg). They feed on plants. It is safe to get near them and see them up close!

The blue-footed booby is a special marine bird. Its blue legs and feet make it easy to recognize. It can be spotted as it **plunge-dives** for fish.

Galapagos carpenter bees are the only bees in the Galapagos. They live throughout the islands. They are important **pollinators** on the islands.

Galapagos racer snakes tend to be dark brown with stripes or spots. They are shy of humans. So, seeing one in the wild can be tough!

Galapagos ghost crabs live on beaches throughout the islands. They can be seen during the day. But they are most active at night when they search for food.

Galapagos fur seals are often spotted on the rocky coasts of James Bay and Darwin Bay. Animal watchers can see pups in the month of October!

Galapagos Islands Experiences

Explore Lava Tunnels
Galapagos National Park

Hike to the Top of an Active Volcano
Isabela Island

Kayak Caves and Coves
Santa Cruz Island

Snorkel with Sea Lions
Santiago Island

Glossary

algae – organisms that live mainly in the water and make their food through photosynthesis. Algae are different from other plants in that they have no leaves, roots, or stems.

habitat – the natural environment of a plant or animal.

plunge-dive – to hunt by diving forcefully into the water to catch fish and other water animals.

pollinator – an insect that carries pollen to a plant, causing the seeds to be fertilized.

species – a group of living things that look alike and can have young together.

Index